If I Could Not Pray

*The Devotional Companion
for All Who Need a Lamp
to Shine Through the Darkness*

Rev. Alfie Wines, Ph.D., Editor

Contributors:

Rev. Dr. Georgia Allen

Rev. Denise Blakely, FLP

Rev. Dr. Jacquetta Chambers

Rev. April Van Rader

Copyright Page

ISBN 978-0999100899

SHEKINAH GLORY
—PUBLISHING—

www.shekinahglorypublishing.org

Please Note

Scripture notations are taken from the translations listed
below and are noted
throughout the text.

- o Amplified Bible (AMP)
- o God's Word (GW)
- o King James Version (KVJ)
- o New American Standard Bible (NASB)
- o New International Version (NIV)
- o New King James Version (NKJV)
- o New Living Translation (NLT)
- o New Revised Standard Version (NRSV)
- o The New Testament in Modern English Translated by
  J. B. Phillips (PHILLIPS)

The masculine pronoun (He, His, Him, etc.) was used for
God, as needed, for a smooth reading of the text.

Dedication

This book is dedicated to Rev. Dr. Georgia Allen,
who paved the way for us.

Pioneers are people who enter and settle a region, territory or position so that others may further develop and occupy these areas. Rev. Dr. Georgia Allen is the pioneer for women in general and minority women in particular who are involved in ministry. She entered the ministry determined to serve God 1st, the United Methodist Church 2nd, and 3rdly, to be an example for clergy women coming after her. She settled the region by inspiring women to be diligent in their preparations, bold in their leadership, and determined in their service to God and the church. Utilizing her skills, strategies, and teachings, clergy women are able to develop their crafts and occupy places of prominence in the United Methodist Church. This devotional book is dedicated to Dr. Georgia Allen as the pioneer for women's ministry. The book is also dedicated to two women who dedicated themselves to seeing that the project matriculated to completion. Rev. Dr. Alfie Wines, Rev. Denise Blakely, & and Rev. April Van Rader kept the fires burning in their own hearts and fanned the embers in the hearts of the other women who submitted devotionals. All of these pioneers, utilized prayer, preparation, and praise to bring forth this work. Ultimately, we dedicate this book to the Glory of God. Without God's grace and mercy, the completion of this book would not be possible. May the God of Goodness & Mercy forever be pleased with this endeavor.

Written by Rev. Dr. Jacquetta Chambers & endorsed by Dr. Alfie Wines, Rev. Denise Blakely & Rev. April Van Raider

With Grateful Hearts

We are grateful to the many people who had a role in this work.
Your love and encouragement made this work possible.

Endorsements

We can learn much about a person by listening to them pray. This prayer journal reflects the prayer journey of five United Methodist clergy women. It gives us a glimpse of their spiritual lives while inviting us to tend to our own spirituality through the gift of prayer. Enjoy the journal; embrace the journey.

Dr. Steve Langford, Senior Pastor
First United Methodist Church Arlington, TX

Dr. Georgia Allen is a servant of God faithfully preaching, continually serving, and making a way where there was no way with grace. As much as she set an example and cleared a path for women, she did it for clergy couples as well. Dr Allen was a pastor and pastor's spouse. In Shonda Rimes terms, Dr Allen is FOD (First Only Different). When you are FOD, everyone is watching, the bar is set high, and excellence is demanded. Dr Georgia Allen understood FOD. The women who write in tribute deliver quality to match. Dr Allen's ministry and this text are like the cup that runs over. Savor the deliciousness offered here. Give thanks for what God has done and continues to do. Thank you, Dr Allen. God bless you.

Rev. Dr. Sarah E. Howe Miller, Ph.D.Pastor, Faith UMC, Fort Worth,
Texas and Asbury UMC, Haltom City, Texas

As one who knows what it feels like to be in a prayer desert, this book is like a tall glass of ice water soothing a thirsty tongue. The reflections are down to earth, full of honesty, and an awareness born from lifetimes spent in relationship with a loving God. Take this balm and rub it on the sore places of your soul. You will find it a gift not just from five faithful clergy sisters, but from the God who holds us in both hands.

Rev. Allyson Paxton, Senior Pastor
Genesis UMC, Fort Worth

I have been the recipient of some of the pray-ers who have written this text - sometimes with sighs too deep for words - the gratitude for which words do not adequately convey. I am honored to call these women colleagues and blessed to have them as friends. They offer a perspective that many of us think we know, but for which we have no grounding for our presumed understanding. I invite each of us to use this book as a resource; that we would open our hearts to listen, to pray with our sisters, to hear their prayers and let the words seep through our skin and into our bones. Let us come alongside and pray with them, honoring their work by using these prayers in worship and personal devotions, giving thanks to God for the gift of their presence in the Central Texas Conference.

Rev. Virginia O. (Ginger) Bassford, PhD
Senior Pastor, St. Barnabas United Methodist Church Arlington, TX

Being a woman in ministry has its many blessings and its many challenges. I know this to be even more true for my clergy sisters of color. I am grateful to Dr. Georgia Allen for her pioneering leadership as the first minority female in the Central Texas Conference. Her pioneering spirit burned a light which the trailblazers who wrote this book followed as they forged paths of their own. Written by clergy women, I hold in high regard, this book offers guidance for a life deeply rooted in prayer. It was beautiful to read and my soul found refreshment in these pages.

Dr. Leah Hidde-Gregory, Central District Superintendent
Central Texas Conference of the United Methodist Church

If I Could Not Pray is truly a labor of love. It is a labor of love honoring their spiritual mentor, the Rev. Dr. Georgia Allen, and it is also a labor of love for the readers who will find their faith renewed. The authors skillfully combine and make accessible the spiritual practices of self-reflection/examen, journaling, scripture and prayer to bring light to one's faith when it finds itself in the catacombs of life. Like the ones who lowered their paralytic friend through the roof to the feet of Jesus' for healing, this guide will do the same when your spirit feels frozen in pain and apathy. It reminds you of the power of simply placing yourself daily at the feet of Jesus. Both individuals and small groups will find this resource helpful.

Rev. Dr. Isabel N. Docampo, Intern Faculty and Director of the
Center for the Study of Latino/a Christianity and Religion
Perkins School of Theology/SMU

The title of this book, **If I Could Not Pray**, is an unusual, yet effective way to focus us on the need to pray. It turns the tables on conventional thinking and invites us to think about why we need pray. Where do we go for healing? How are we going to respond when a relationship is broken? To whom do we go for forgiveness for our self or to find the capacity to forgive others? Where do we find strength? How do we tap into the wellsprings of joy, of courage, or of wisdom? These five clergywomen take us on journey of faith and discovery revealing the power that prayer provides. Based on their experiences they become our guides. The scriptures they have selected and the personal commentary they provide, prompt us to use the daily journal for reflection and prayer. It is a helpful resource for any pilgrim.

Dr. Bob Holloway, Retired East District Superintendent,
Dean of the Cabinet of the Central Texas
Conference of the United Methodist Church

Preface for *If I Could Not Pray*

A group of top flight female pastors and theologians from the Central Texas Annual Conference have collaborated on a superb little book about prayer. In a series of essays, they have explored scripture and their inner humanity to offer us new perspectives on prayer.

Some people think of prayer as sweet, well-spoken words addressed to God to do our will. When Jesus speaks of prayer Jesus suggests what Fred Craddock describes in a sermon titled: "Praying through Clenched Teeth." Prayer is not so much prayer retreats, meditation, the lotus position, or having proper words or posture. No, according to Jesus, prayer is more like beating on heaven's door until someone answers. It is prayer that is so persistent and tenacious that even the most reluctant finally surrenders because he or she knows the one knocking is certainly not going to give up or give in. Prayer is "the Persistent Widow" (see: Luke 18:1-8)!

Prayer is a fascinating topic for most of us. Many people have strong opinions about prayer. Some say "Pray continually" (1 Thessalonians 5:17). These authors of *If I Could Not Pray* write:

Pray in season and out of season. Pray when times are good and pray when times are bad. Pray when you feel like it and pray when you don't feel like it. Pray silently and pray out loud. Pray alone and pray with others. The easiest thing you will ever do is . . . pray. The hardest thing you will ever do is . . . pray.

Prayer seems like an easy concept to grasp and yet how many people fail to pray simply because they do not know where to begin. Even a disciple asked Jesus, "Lord, teach us to pray, just as John taught his disciples" (Luke 11:1).

I urge you, as a voice urged Saint Augustine so long ago, "Take up and read; Take up and read" [Tolle, lege! Tolle, lege!]. This little book will help guide you into one of the most fundamental Christian spiritual disciplines that you may ever practice.

Rev. David Neil Mosser
Senior Pastor, First United Methodist Church,
Salado, Texas

Foreword
by
Rev. Roderick Miles

If I Could Not Pray is one of the most refreshing answers to the Body of Christ's critical need for fellowship with God. These reflections contain valuable lessons on prayer for everyday living in a warm, personal form. Many will draw inspiration from these reflections that will encourage all who dare to grow closer to God.

Why do we need to know so much about prayer? That's simple. As long as Christians are living defeated lives with the wealth and power of God a prayer away, we need a word on prayer. Maybe an observation from my career in commissioned sales will help paint the picture.

Commissioned sales people as a group are some of the wealthiest and poorest members of the North American workforce. I know that sounds strange, but it's true. There are two basic reasons for this phenomenon: First, most commercial customers make the decision to make major purchases after the fifth attempt to close a sale, and secondly, around 80% of all sales people know only two ways to close a sale and use only one method well. The reason for the wide range of income is simple—knowledge of sales closing methods.

The Bible says that God's people perish for lack of knowledge, including, knowledge of prayer. Between "Now I lay me down to sleep . . ." and The Lord's Prayer (which is really just a model for prayer) we have exhausted the prayer arsenal of many Christians. The Church is anemic in its prayer life and as a result, impotent in its life.

I believe that by taking to heart the messages offered in this devotional, your fellowship with God our Father will be enhanced and your life as a believer enriched.

Rev. Roderick F. Miles
Retired District Superintendent
Central Texas Conference
United Methodist Church Fort Worth, TX

A Word from the Editor

Pray without ceasing. Pray in season and out of season. Pray when times are good. Pray when times are bad. Pray when you feel like it. Pray when you don't feel like it. Pray silently. Pray out loud. Pray alone. Pray with others. The easiest thing you'll ever do is . . . pray. The hardest thing you'll ever do is . . . pray.

There have been times in my life when I was so hungry for God, I couldn't wait to get home to pray. There have been times when I went to sleep praying and times when I awoke praying. There have been times when my prayers were answered immediately and times when it seemed like the answers would never come. There have been times when I didn't want the prayer to end as I prayed in silence and lingered in the peace and rest of God. At times, the hurt was so deep all I could do was weep aloud. Sometimes my prayer was a dance or a song. Sometimes when I'm at the piano, my song is a prayer. Sometimes, I'm so happy, my laughter is my prayer. Even in my dry spells, I long to pray.

Yes, believe it or not, even pastors have dry spells. There are times when God seems far away. Times when it seems God has forgotten. Times when it seems that time with God and God's Word is just another item on a "To Do" list that is much too full. Times when prayer and/or reading the Bible is uninviting, uninspiring, and unrewarding—in other words, it's the last thing you want to do. Yet, even with dry spells, I find that somehow my need for God calls me. God pulls at my heartstrings until I respond. God pulls at my heartstrings and then I remember the words of a gospel song I learned years ago, "Jesus is on the main line, tell him what you want . . . call him up and tell him what you want."

Through prayer I have been relieved of burdens untold. Through prayer I've discovered new possibilities for my life. Through prayer I've been convicted and corrected more times than I can count. Through prayer, my I've found renewal for my sagging soul. Through prayer, I've learned to face difficult times with faith instead of fear. I often wonder, "What would I do if I could not pray?"

Yet, the truth is, it hasn't always been this way. When I look back two things amaze me. First, I've only been excited about prayer for about twenty years. Now don't get me wrong, my parents taught me to pray since before I can remember. Yet, it has only been since 1994 that I finally learned to take my prayer life out of the box. What a difference it has made in my life! Sometimes, all I can do is say, "Wow! Look at what God as done!"

Second, although I spent years studying Biblical Interpretation, Christian Living, and related topics for a long time I had absolutely no interest in books on prayer. I'm one of those people who can spend hours in a bookstore. Sometimes, I even have a "bookstore day" when I visit several of my favorite bookstores perusing the aisles and selecting my favorites. Somehow, books on prayer never caught my attention.

Sometimes the power of a good conversation can lead us to new directions in our lives. It was a summer day in July of 1994 and I was on the phone with Mrs. Reese Barnett. At the time, I was the facilitator of an Adult Sunday School class at Carter Metropolitan CME Church in Fort Worth, TX. Her husband, Mr. John Barnett, was a participant in the group. I had called to tell him about an upcoming class event. He wasn't at home. I thought I was going to leave a quick message with Mrs. Barnett and get on with the rest of my day. Instead, Mrs. Barnett and I started talking and she shared her heart for prayer with me. Two hours later, I couldn't wait to purchase the book she'd recommended, *Prayer,* by O. Hallesby.

Reading Hallesby's book made me realize that there was more to prayer than just routinely saying my prayers on my knees at night before bedtime. Soon, I was reading every book on prayer that I could find including John Killinger's book, *Beginning Prayer* which introduced me a whole new realm of prayer. During this period, I also learned that my Dad prayed for me twice a day since before I was born! I wondered, "Where have I been all these years?"

My how my life has changed! When my interest in scripture (which began in 1978 when I returned to church after a ten-year hiatus) and my interest in prayer began to merge, I had no idea that God was leading me on a path toward ministry.

Along the way, God has blessed me with many wonderful clergywomen who share this journey in ministry from many denominations along the way. Among them are the clergywomen of the Central Texas Conference of the United Methodist Church. What began ten years ago as a solo project has blossomed into a corporate project shared by the five Central Texas clergywomen whose work appears in this volume.

As we prayed about this project, our prayer was that many would be blessed by our work. Your reading this volume is a fulfillment of this prayer. May God hear and answer your prayers. May God bless you a hundredfold and keep you always in his care.

Rev. Alfie Wines, Ph.D.

For the Reader

Life is a wonderful gift. God gives us the awesome privilege and the awesome responsibility of determining much of the who, what, when, where, how and why of our lives. Even in the midst of the "issues, problems and challenges" of everyday life, God is good, life is good. One of the psalmists reminds us:

No good thing will the LORD withhold from those who do what is right.

Psalm 84:11b (NLT)

May God increase the good things in your life a hundredfold.

As you begin, our prayer for you is:

> *In times of trouble, may the Lord respond to your cry.*
>
> *May the God of Israel keep you safe from all harm.*
>
> *May He send you help from his sanctuary and strengthen you from*
>
> > *Jerusalem.*
>
> *May He remember all your gifts and look favorably on your burnt offerings.*
>
> *May He grant your heart's desire and fulfill all your plans.*

May we shout for joy when we hear of your victory,

flying banners to honor our God.

May the Lord answer all your prayers!

Psalm 20:1-5 (NLT)

The Clergywomen,
Rev. Dr. Georgia Allen
Rev. Denise Blakely, FLP
Rev. Dr. Jacquetta Chambers
Rev. April Van Rader
Rev. Alfie Wines, Ph.D.

Before You Begin . . .

Life gets more and more complex every day. There's an endless round of people to see, places to go, things to do. Hurry, hurry. Faster, faster. These are the unspoken mottoes of the day. The pace of our lives allows us to have a higher standard of living, but it also increases the stress in our lives. We are so busy we do not even realize how stressed out, how unbalanced we really are. Like the congregation in Laodicea, we don't realize the deception, the distortion with which we live when we say to ourselves, "I'm wealthy, I don't need anything" (Rev. 3:17a, God's Word). Yet, the truth of the matter is that, like the church at Laodicea, we do not "realize that . . . (we) are miserable, pitiful, poor, blind, and naked" (Rev. 3:17b, God's Word).

If we slow down, even for a moment, we begin to notice a gap between the quantity and the quality of our lives. We begin to ask ourselves, "What's missing?" Sooner or later, in our hearts, we begin to recognize that truth is missing. The writer of Isaiah says it this way:

Truth has fallen in the street, and honesty can't come in. Truth is missing." (Isaiah 59:14-15a God's Word)

In these moments of seeking truth we begin to examine the quality of our lives—we examine our relationships with God, others and ourselves, and what we do with our "time, talents and treasures." As we begin to seek the truth that is missing, we look at our spiritual lives. If we are honest with ourselves, we will recognize a spiritual void.

Look in any bookstore and you'll find more books and magazine articles on spirituality than ever before. Look at any television or radio schedule and you'll find more stations and programs devoted to spiritual issues than ever before. And it's not just the religious stations. We see it on the major television and public broadcasting stations as well. People from all walks of life are searching for meaning in their lives.

Ultimately, this examination leads us to look for God. And if we look for God, the success of our search is guaranteed, for God promised that if we look for him, we will find him. God promised to reveal himself to us. Jeremiah 29:13-4a reads: "When you look for me, you will find me. When you wholeheartedly seek me, I will let you find me" (God's Word). God seeks us and gives us the desire to seek Him. Our seeking him is a sign that He is seeking us. The responses to this cry of the spirit are infinite.

If I Could Not Pray consists of prayerful reflections of five clergywomen who serve the United Methodist Church. Drawn together by their passion for prayer, in this book we share our passion with you. Our prayers reflect the rhythm of life, good days, bad days, and days in-between.

The writers know that sometimes when we come to God, our stay is brief. Other times, we linger, enjoying the peace of his presence. There are times when we have much to pray about. Other times we seek just a brief moment with God. Still others are times of deep lengthy reflection. These reflections mirror those various types of time with God.

Take a break from your busy life. Sit back, relax, and enjoy these reflections. Enjoy your time with God. Perhaps as you read, you too may find yourself wondering, "What Would I Do If I Could Not Pray?"

The Clergywomen,
Rev. Dr. Georgia Allen
Rev. Denise Blakely, FLP
Rev. Dr. Jacquetta Chambers
Rev. April Van Rader
Rev. Alfie Wines, Ph.D.

Table of Contents

Appendix

If I Could Not Pray

May the words of my mouth and the thoughts of my heart,

(and the writings on my computer!)

be pleasing to you, O Lord,

my Rock and my Redeemer.

Psalm 19:14 (NLT)

What is This Thing Called Prayer?

What is this thing called prayer? Prayer is a means of opening ourselves to God. It is a means of connecting with God whom we "address . . . in word or thought (or silence)" (Webster's New Collegiate Dictionary, 1973) and listen for God's response. In prayer, we talk with God about himself,[1] others, and ourselves.

Prayer is one way of loving God, others, and ourselves. When we learn to pray about everything, prayer time can be the best part of our day. Learning to pray about everything can be the starting point that brings unity and focus to the complexity of our lives. Our prayers cover a tremendous variety of topics. The variety is so great, that the idea of praying about everything can be a bit overwhelming. Yet, this is just what God (through the writings of Paul) encourages and commands us to do.

Always be joyful in the Lord! I'll say it again: Be joyful! Let everyone know how considerate you are. The Lord is near. Never worry about anything. But in every situation let God know what you need in prayers and requests while giving thanks. Then God's peace, which goes beyond anything we can imagine will guard your thoughts and emotions through Christ Jesus.

Philippians 4:4-8 God's Word

---

[1]God is spirit without reference to gender. Occasional references to God in gender language is due to linguistic limitations of the English language.

God did not put any restrictions on prayer. God is open to any topic that is in our hearts and on our minds. We can pray silently, out loud, with words, without words, in words we understand, in words we don't understand, with moans and groans, with tears, with laughter. We can pray standing, sitting, kneeling, laying down, with hands upraised, with our faces to the ground. We can pray with our eyes open. We can pray with our eyes closed. We can pray in private, we can pray in public. We can pray during special times set aside for prayer. We can pray short prayers. We can pray long prayers. We can pray in the midst of daily activities. We can pray anytime, anywhere.

Like the disciples who asked Jesus to teach them to pray, we too can look at the life of Jesus and learn much about prayer. Jesus is the best example of the difference prayer can make in one's life. What was it about him that made his life so powerful that people left familiar lives to follow an itinerant preacher? What is it that made his life so powerful his words speak to us throughout the ages? It was his awareness of his spirituality, his connection to God, his prayer life that made the difference in his life. Prayer can make a difference in our lives too. When we make prayer a regular part of our lives we'll be amazed at what God can do. Let the power and peace of God wash over you as you read and meditate on these reflections.

If I Could Not Pray

Rev. Alfie Wines, Ph.D.

(In memory of my friend, Luella Hopkins Gulley)

Scripture:

As the deer pants for streams of water, so I long for you, O God. Ps. 42:1 NLT

Reflection:

O, Lord, my God, what would I do if I could not pray?

In the midst of cell phones, traffic, voice-mail, e-mail, texts, family, work, bills . . .

I need your gentleness, your presence, your peace, your love.

On days like today, what would I do if I could not pray?

It's frightening that you know me so well—my sins, my faults, and my failures.

Impossible as it is, sometimes I want to hide even from you.

And yet, it's reassuring that though you know all this about me, you ***never*** use it against me.

I'm glad that when my uncertainty, my insecurity, and my questions surface,

you remind me of who I am despite my shortcomings. You remind me that I am

a beloved daughter, that I am made in the image, in the likeness of you.

Thank you for reminding me that even there are so many things awry in the world, even

when things are awry in my life

You encourage me, assuring me that the day will surely come when your image in me is whole, full and complete.

Thank you for your faithfulness, for the love and healing that time spent with you brings

On days like today, when things fall apart, what would I do if I could not pray?

Thank you, Lord Jesus, for going through the worst to open new vistas of life for me.

You are, indeed, the truest of friends.

Thank You for being my Creator, my Redeemer, my Sustainer, my Helper, my Friend.

Thank You for your constant presence, for being available, for listening, for sticking with me through it all, through good days, bad days, and days in-between.

On days like today, what would I do if I could not pray?

Reflection Question:

Imagine what your life would be like if you could not pray. Take time to thank God for prayer.

_____
_____
_____
_____
_____
_____
_____
_____
_____

_____
_____
_____
_____
_____
_____
_____
_____
_____
_____
_____
_____
_____
_____
_____
_____
_____
_____
_____
_____
_____
_____
_____
_____
_____
_____
_____
_____
_____
_____

Prayer:

God, where are you? Where are you? Sometimes you seem so distant and far away. I confess my need for you. In the midst of my chaos, in the midst of it all, I need you. Just for a moment, help me stop, collect my thoughts, and focus on you. What would I do if I could not pray?

God's Great Creation

Rev. Dr. Georgia Allen

Scripture:

In the beginning God created the heaven and the earth.
Genesis 1:1 KJV

Reflection:

Traveling along our beautiful highways this summer, my family and I felt especially blessed as we just looked about surveying the benefits and attractions of the lush countryside as we passed along. There were nice rest stops with beautiful landscaping and clean comfortable surroundings. From time to time we would stroll around for a bit just stretching our legs.

Soon we came upon this soothing scene complete with picnic tables under luscious shade trees. As we lingered sitting and talking we could feel the cool breezes stirring the leaves and our senses. Suddenly, we felt a surge of appreciation and gratitude to God for this beautiful world—a surge we seldom felt because we rarely take time to enjoy nature. It made us want to say, "Thanks be to God for this wonderful creation. Thank you, God, that through nature you have generously provided for our every need. As we talked about the creativity, forethought, and loving care that went into making this beautiful world we were reminded that we benefit by sharing in the mighty creative plan of God. Before we knew it we were thanking God for the moment that brought us to this place   at this time in our lives. What a privilege it is to worship and praise our awesome God!

Reflection Questions:

What are some of your memorable experiences when you paid special attention to the beauty of nature? Did the experiences cause you to marvel at the handiwork of God?

_____
_____
_____
_____
_____
_____
_____
_____
_____
_____
_____
_____
_____
_____
_____
_____
_____
_____
_____

Prayer:

Thank you, Lord, for all your blessings! Give me a heart to appreciate the wonder of your creation and a spirit tuned to your great plan for my life.

Standing Firm

Rev. Dr. Georgia Allen

Scripture:

Blessed is the man Who walks not in the counsel of the ungodly, Nor stands in the path of sinners, Nor sits in the seat of the scornful; but his delight is in the law of the LORD, And in His law he meditates day and night. He shall be like a tree Planted by the rivers of water, That brings forth its fruit in its season, Whose leaf also shall not wither; And whatever he does shall prosper. The ungodly are not so But are like the chaff which the wind drives away. Therefore, the ungodly shall not stand in the judgment, Nor sinners in the congregation of the righteous. For the LORD knows the way of the righteous, But the way of the ungodly shall perish. Psalm 1:1-5 NKJV

Reflection:

Life can be full of great ups and great downs as any of us can attest to. With God on our side we are more than conquerors over the volatile circumstances of life. With God, we can be as steady as a tree planted by rivers of water in the midst of the unpredictability of today's world.

People often say, "You just cannot depend on anything in this world today." We know; however, this is not true. With God in our corner, we can rest assured that we are ok, that everything is going to be alright--no matter what life throws our way! The Psalmist said, "If it had not been for the Lord on my side where would I be, where would I be." We stand firm each day buoyed by the presence of God and encouraged by the matchless care of God. We stand firm in knowledge of the keeping power of our God.

Thanks be to God! He has made us like trees planted by the rivers of water. Confident in God, we know we can, will and do stand firm and unmovable, bearing good fruit in the name of the Lord.

Reflection Questions:

Are you planted, well-watered, and bearing good fruit? If not, what do you plan to do about it?

_____
_____
_____
_____
_____
_____
_____

Prayer:

Lord, make me fruitful in your service. Make me faithful and steadfast in your work. Help me stay planted, rooted and grounded in you. May I always take time to be watered by your Word. Let me bear good fruit as I invest in the lives of others. Let me bear good fruit as I go about the ordinary business of everyday living.

Get Dressed

Rev. Dr. Georgia Allen

Scripture:

Finally, my brethren, be strong in the Lord and in the power of His might. Put on the whole armor of God, that you may be able to stand against the wiles of the devil. Ephesians: 6:10-11NKJV

Reflection:

Almost everyone likes to dress up. Even when we don't like to dress up, we still like to look nice, don't we? Well, my friends, unfortunately, we sometimes place far too much emphasis on how we look instead of a more substantial reality. It is good to look good, yes, it is, but it is far more important to be good. We think that if our actions rival our looks we are ok, right? When we dress for the service of the Lord our looks must be attractive *and* useful.

Our armor must be practical and visible for, whether we realize it or not, we are in a life and death battle with the invisible forces of evil. Our behavior must give visible evidence of our inner spirit. Our behavior is the clothing we wear.

If you have been lax, it is time to put your clothes on. Go on now, get dressed. Time is wasting. We have a lot to accomplish! Our Lord is depending on us to cover and protect ourselves while we do serious battle with the enemy. The enemy can engage you at any moment in the battle of your life (and for your life). We must be ready at all times.

Come on now! Get dressed! Get dressed! It is time to fight on the Lord's side.

Reflection Question:

Are you dressed for the battle, i.e. the challenges of everyday living? If not, why not? If not, what must you do to make sure that you are always properly dressed?

_____
_____
_____
_____
_____
_____
_____
_____
_____

Prayer:

Thank you, Lord, for equipping me, for giving me all I need for victory in my life. I know that you want the best for me. I know that you are on my side. Give me strength and courage to do what I need to do when I need to do it for the right reason. Thank you, Lord, that you are with me, equipping me, always.

Just Keep Standing!!

Rev. Dr. Georgia Allen

Scripture:

Stand fast therefore in the liberty wherewith Christ hath made us free and be not entangled again with the yoke of bondage. Galatians 5:1 KJV

Reflection:

Stand up for right, stand up for God! God rules this world. And, yes, he rules with truth and grace, with power and tender care. Make no mistake about it, God does rule. We, God's human creatures, often forget or are seduced into splitting our allegiance vacillating between right and wrong, good and bad. We are admonished in God's word that we are to stand firm in the things of God. Don't give place to the devil. Don't grow weary. We are told also that when we have done all to stand, stand. Stand, therefore. How about that? God has great expectations for us we know but, can we say the same?

My sisters and brothers stop dallying. Just do it! Stand!!!

Reflection Question:

What do you do to take a stand for God?

_____

_____

_____

_____

_____

Prayer:

Thank you; Lord for the grace to stand, to be a person of integrity in every situation. I give you thanks for helping me stand today.

Let Us Pray

Rev. Dr. Georgia Allen

Scripture:

Our Father who art in heaven, Hallowed be Thy name.

Thy kingdom come, Thy will be done on earth as it is in heaven.

Give us this day our daily bread, and forgive us our trespasses

  as we forgive those who trespass against us.

And lead us not into temptation but deliver us from evil.

For thine is the kingdom and the power and the glory forever.

Luke 11: 1-13 (Also see Matthew 6:9-13)

Reflection:

The prayer that our Lord taught His disciples touches the whole scope of human need and gives voice to the praise and worship our Lord deserves. God wants our praise. The Word tells us that God actually inhabits the praises of His people. Isn't that rich? When we pray we must be very careful to give God praise first and then we make our wants and wishes known. Scripture teaches us that Christians should always pray. Prayer is a powerful tool in the hands of the believer. Prayer changes things! Yes, it does! Make time to talk with the Lord every day and as many times a day as you're led—short prayers, long prayers, whatever you need. Lift others up in prayer. Don't pray just for yourself. May God bless you as you take time to enrich your prayer life.

Reflection Question:

Do you regularly mix praise and thanksgiving with your petitions? If not, make sure that every petition is accompanied by praise and thanksgiving.

_____
_____
_____
_____
_____
_____
_____
_____
_____
_____
_____
_____
_____
_____
_____
_____
_____
_____
_____
_____
_____
_____
_____
_____
_____
_____

Prayer:

Lord, teach me to pray.

When Things Go Wrong

Rev. Dr. Georgia Allen

Scripture:

And my God will meet all your needs according to his glorious riches in Christ Jesus. Philippians 4:19 NIV

Reflection:

It seems that Murphy's Law works overtime at the most inconvenient times. Indeed, sometimes it seems that everything that can go wrong will go wrong." Have you ever had a really good day when spoiler showed up, seemingly from nowhere.

We've all had those days. The babysitter is sick and cannot come in today. Meanwhile, you have an important meeting that has taken you weeks to get all the parties lined up. You really do not need to miss this meeting. You could ask a friend to cover for you, but when you call, you find that the friend who could help is also sick today. "What should I do?" you wonder. It is too late to cancel, so you call your sister to keep your little one while you head off to your important meeting. Now, you owe her a favor the time and place to be decided by her in her own time. You are on the hook, but what must be must be. Then you get to your office, you discover that the principal for your meeting has had to cancel also. So, now you went to work just to learn you did not to have go through all that trouble since your meeting was cancelled anyway! Now to top it off, you still owe your sister big time. By the way, the babysitter called to say her headache is so much better now, and she wants to know if you want her to come in! On days like this, anything that can go wrong will go wrong.

Finally, you quiet yourself long enough to realize you're glad that everyone is ok. As you start to count your blessing in the situation, you learn that your boss has decided to give you that promotion you put in for a month ago and all is well. Aren't you glad you simply adjusted your day and you didn't make a fuss. Aren't you glad you held your peace! Thank you, Holy Spirit, for helping me to be patient today! Yes, all is well!

Reflection Questions:

What do you do when things go wrong during your day? Do you get flustered and bent out of shape? Do you slow down, catch your breath, and regroup? Do you ask God to help you be patient?

_____
_____
_____
_____
_____
_____
_____
_____
_____
_____
_____

_____
_____
_____
_____
_____
_____
_____
_____
_____
_____
_____
_____
_____
_____
_____
_____
_____
_____
_____
_____
_____
_____
_____
_____
_____
_____
_____
_____
_____
_____
_____
_____

<u>Prayer:</u>

Thank you, Lord, for taking care of all my needs today according to your riches in glory by Christ Jesus. With a grateful heart, I pray.

Just Relax

Rev. Dr. Georgia Allen

Scriptures:

Trust in the LORD with all your heart and lean not on your own understanding; in all your

ways acknowledge him, and he will direct your paths. Proverbs 3:5-6 NIV

Come near to God and he will come near to you. Wash your hands, you sinners, and

purify your hearts, you double-minded. James 4:8 NIV

Reflection:

Today I am writing this while I'm on vacation relaxing with friends, doing just what I want to do, when I want to it, exactly in the way that I want. I'm sitting here at the finest barbecue restaurant in Texas (I'll never tell . . . you'll just have to guess!) breaking bread together with friends.

It is good to be able to put our cares aside and just sit back, relax, and know that all is well. Vacation and relaxation are wonderful tools that we all can use to model our behavior in everyday life. In our fast-paced world we are accustomed to being on edge--so much of the time that the very idea of relaxing, even relaxing in the Lord, takes some getting used to.

The Word urges us to "cast all our cares on him for he cares for us. It is so rare that we're given time (or take the time) to just do nothing but work on our attitude. With constant noise from people and media of every sort, we need to revamp our mindset, our world view on a regular basis.

Use your down time wisely. Use it to realign your life plan. Use it to reflect the presence and lordship of Jesus and how his lordship should affect your every word, thought, and deed. Do this and you'll find that you can relax in the Lord. Relax. God will take care of you.

Reflection Questions:

When was the last time you took some time to relax in God? What did you do? How did you feel? What new insights did you have?

_____
_____
_____
_____
_____
_____
_____
_____
_____

Prayer:

Dear God, teach me to trust you more. Teach me how to simply relax in You and give You dominion in my life in every way and at all times.

Then and Now

Rev. Dr. Georgia Allen

Scripture:

Forget the former things; do not dwell on the past. See, I am doing a new thing! Now it springs up; do you not perceive it? I am making a way in the desert and streams in the wasteland. Isaiah 43:18-19 NIV

Reflection:

In the small southeast Texas town where I grew up, life was very different from how it is where I live today. I am sure it was partly due to the time I grew up in and partly due to the climate of live in our town. For instance, we were present in Sunday school and morning worship every Sunday. We were present on Sunday evening for young people's training and evening service. At least once during the week and sometimes twice, we would go to the church again. You say, "Oh, that was a different time and different era, so yes and no, what could you expect?" Life is rarely that simple. That was my experience, but not everyone's experience was the same.

As a little girl, I loved church. I loved the Lord. I benefited from the preaching and teaching at my church. There were others who did not regard the church and did not know the Lord. Generally, however, God was central in my community. I would like to think that the atmosphere of holiness and commitment could somehow be central in our communities today. It seems, though, that every effort is being made to lessen the influence of Christ and his church in the affairs of the world today. Everybody and everything seems to be in competition for the minds and hearts of our young people. God forbid that this atmosphere should prevail. We need the Lord and we need the church; we need Christian men and women who will be examples of a Holy God at work in our lives. We are called to be witnesses sharing God's good news to the world. We cannot turn back the hands of time, but we can influence the places where we live here and now.

Reflection Questions:

What differences have you seen in life then and now? What do you think made the difference? What do you need to let go of from yesterday? What do you need embrace to make room for today?

_____
_____
_____
_____
_____
_____
_____

Prayer:

Lord, let me be a good witness for you wherever I am and in whatever I do. Thank you for the privilege of serving you. Let me understand the difference between then and now. Help me let go of the things I need to let go of from yesterday. Help me embrace what I need to embrace for abundant living today and tomorrow.

Let Love Abide

Rev. Dr. Georgia Allen

Scripture:

If ye keep my commandments, ye shall abide in my love; even as I have kept my Father's commandments and abide in his love. John 15:10 KJV

Reflection:

The old deacon would pray "Oh gracious and almighty God, let your love abide, let it reach from heart to heart and from breast to breast." The church would swell with exclamations of loud "Yes, Lord" and "Please, Jesus" and Thank you, Father!" The very atmosphere would be pregnant with the presence and love of God. "What a privilege and a blessing," we would sing, "to be in the house of the Lord."

When we set the tone for worship in the house of the Lord, when we praise and magnify the Lord, we can be sure that the Holy Spirit will be present to teach and empower us to love one another. We are told in the word that the presence of the Lord inhabits the praises of His people. Where two or three are gathered in His name he promised to be in the midst. I am so grateful that God is with us in whatever we do, in our going out and our coming in. We are blessed indeed in the presence of the Lord.

If I could share a word with you today, it would be this, "Open your heart to the Lord and let him have full sway in your life. Praise and honor Him with your all. He loves you and is worthy of your praise. Love God and love one another. God is depending on you to extend his influence wherever he sends you. Let your praises go up. Let love abide.

Reflection Questions:

What is the connection between praise and love? How do you let love abide? How do you stop the flow of God's love? What must you do in order to praise God and let love abide even more?

_____
_____
_____
_____
_____
_____
_____
_____
_____
_____
_____
_____
_____
_____

Prayer:

O Gracious and Almighty God let your love abide and let it reach from heart to heart and from breast to breast. Help me do my part to let your love flow in the world today.

His Goodness and Mercy

Rev. Dr. Georgia Allen

Scripture:

Read Psalm 23 below at least two times. Then you may read on.

The LORD is my shepherd; I shall not want. He makes me to lie down in green pastures; He leads me beside the still waters. He restores my soul; He leads me in the paths of righteousness For His name's sake. Yea, though I walk through the valley of the shadow of death, I will fear no evil; For You are with me; Your rod and Your staff, they comfort me. You prepare a table before me in the presence of my enemies; You anoint my head with oil; My cup runs over. Surely goodness and mercy shall follow me. All the days of my life; And I will dwell in the house of the LORD forever. Psalm 23 NKJV

Reflection:

Almost every child knows of this psalm and most can recite it from memory. As adults, however, we tend to remember the words while treating it as some almost forgotten bit of our early training that simply remains just a memorized passage of scripture. It's time to remember. It's time to give attention to the underlying message of this Psalm.

When we prayerfully engage the 23rd Psalm, we are comforted, we are informed of God's care, and we are strengthened in every way. This Psalm is a favorite of many, many believers. On several occasions I've had the opportunity to teach and preach on this passage. It is often requested for funeral sermons. Every phrase seems to wrap itself around the reader, whispering words of love and hope. We are reminded that God's goodness and mercy will truly see us through every circumstance. Surely, goodness and mercy will follow each of us for the rest of our earthly life and beyond.

Reflection Questions:

Take a few moments to meditate on this psalm. Bow your head now and whisper a word of prayer right where you are? Who is God to you? Why not write your own 23rd Psalm?

_____

_____

_____

_____

_____

_____

_____

_____

_____

_____

_____

_____

_____

_____

_____

Prayer:

Lord, give me an attitude of gratitude for all the goodness and mercy that you show me every day. I thank you, Lord, for giving us this wonderful psalm.

Zacchaeus

Rev. April Van Rader

Scripture:

When Jesus reached the spot, He looked up and said to him, "Zacchaeus, come down immediately. I must stay at your house today." Luke 19:5 NIV

Reflection:

Jesus was entering Jericho when He spotted Zacchaeus in the sycamore tree; for Zacchaeus, getting a glimpse of Jesus through the crowd was difficult because he was of short stature. Jesus kept His word and dined at the tax collector's home. Sometime during dinner, Zacchaeus stood up and proclaimed that he had repented and was going to give half of his possessions away and pay back four times what he had stolen! Jesus said of Zacchaeus, "today salvation has come to this house." Not only would Zacchaeus' life change, the lives of those who received fourfold what he had stolen would be changed also.

Even though Zacchaeus was a despised tax collector who amassed wealth at the expense of others, Jesus saw the heart of the man and was able to reach Zacchaeus at his point of need, for he needed salvation. The scripture states that Zacchaeus was of short stature, it is interesting that the Bible makes direct reference to Zacchaeus' height. Was he ridiculed because he was shorter in stature than most men? Was swindling the wealthy and overtaxing the needy his way of getting back at others because of how he was treated? Jesus comes on the scene and spots Zacchaeus in the tree. The Messiah publicly declares that he has chosen to spend an evening at this man's house, which affirms him in a way no one else ever could! After spending time with Jesus, Zacchaeus finds the love and acceptance he has always been looking for and the forgiveness that he needs in the eyes of his Creator; this man Zacchaeus was never the same again.

Reflection Questions:

Imagine Jesus coming to your house for dinner. How do you feel? What does Jesus inspire you to do that changes your life? How might this change in your life have a positive effect in the lives of others? Despite any imperfections you may have, what affirmations have you received after spending quality time with the Lord?

_____
_____
_____
_____
_____
_____
_____
_____
_____
_____
_____
_____
_____
_____
_____
_____

_____
_____
_____
_____
_____
_____
_____
_____
_____
_____
_____
_____
_____
_____
_____
_____
_____
_____
_____
_____
_____
_____
_____
_____
_____
_____
_____
_____

Prayer:

Thank you, Lord, that in spite of our faults and failures, you are still willing to visit us where we live. Come into my house today, Lord. Come into my heart. Change my life, change my heart today.

New Beginnings

Rev. April Van Rader

Scripture:

So if anyone is in Christ, there is a new creation: everything old has passed away; see, everything has become new! 2 Corinthians 5:17 NIV

Reflection:

A fresh start; different from the first part; never used source. This is the way *that The American Heritage Dictionary* defines the words NEW and BEGINNINGS. The Bible's definition of New Beginnings is found in 2 Corinthians 5:17; it reads "So if anyone is in Christ, there is a new creation: everything old has passed away; see, everything has become new!"

Aren't you glad that God is a God of second chances? A God of new beginnings whenever we need them as we travel life's highway. Jesus' command to forgive seventy times seven is a reminder that God's mercy is so great that we are allowed to begin again—and again and again—and that we should extend that same mercy to others. When Jesus told Nicodemus, an age

d teacher of the Law of Moses, that he needed to be "born again" he was telling him that he had to have a new beginning.

Jesus taught that God's forgiveness is the key to starting over. God's forgiveness transforms our lives just as if we'd *NEVER* sinned. How many times have you asked God to forgive you, to give you a new beginning? Seventy times seven and even more than you can count. How many times must you forgive your sister or brother? Seventy times seven. . ... that's the path to a new beginning.

Reflection Questions*:*

Today is the first day of the rest of your life. In what area(s) of your life do you need to ask God's forgiveness so that you can have a fresh start today? Who do you need to forgive so that both you and they can move on (together or apart) in order to have a new beginning today?

_____
_____
_____
_____
_____
_____
_____
_____
_____
_____
_____
_____

Prayer:

Today, Lord, forgive me for thoughts, words, and deeds in my life that are not according to your will and your way. I want to be born again, freed in mind and spirit because you have forgiven me. Help me extend that same freedom to everyone.

A Sturdy Grasp

Rev. April Van Rader

Scripture:

For I am persuaded that neither death, nor life, nor angels, nor principalities, nor powers, nor things present, nor things to come, nor height, nor depth, nor any other creature shall be able to separate us from the love of God which is in Christ Jesus." Romans 8:38-39 KJV

Reflection:

Sometimes in our self-chastisement, we feel that we have strayed too far from God, sinned too many times, or denied Christ too often to be forgiven. We can always count on the enemy to help by reminding us of what we've done, how far we've fallen, and how frequently we've missed the mark. However, God's Word says that we can't run fast enough, sink low enough, or travel far enough (even to the depths of hell) from God's love for us which is in Christ Jesus. A songwriter wrote that we should hold on to God's unchanging hand; not only is God's hand strong enough to hold us when we're falling, God's grasp is sturdy enough to lift us up and keep us standing firm! Sometimes we sink so low that the mountaintop we're trying to reach is only the sidewalk. We must remember that the echo from the bottom of the barrel is the loudest! Even in our worst state, God sees us, hears us, and loves us. God will dig us up out of the barrel and help us to reach the stars!

Reflection Question:

Do you recall a specific instance in your life where you really appreciated the sturdy grasp that God had on you, even when you were at the bottom of a barrel? Give God thanks for the steady grasp that has never left you alone.

_____
_____
_____
_____
_____
_____
_____
_____
_____
_____
_____
_____
_____
_____
_____
_____
_____
_____
_____
_____
_____
_____
_____

Prayer:

Thank you God for your steady grasp—the grasp that holds me even when my life is falling apart. Remind me that even when I feel alone and distant from you, the truth is that nothing, absolutely nothing, can separate me from your love which is in Christ Jesus.

Trust God

Rev. April Van Rader

Scripture:

Trust in the LORD with all your heart and lean not on your own understanding; in all your ways acknowledge him, and he will direct your paths. Proverbs 3:5-6 NIV

Reflection:

We know that God can handle our big problems, but we still stress ourselves out worrying about the little ones. Scripture reminds us that God will handle all of our problems if we allow Him to do so. We offend God when we give credit to someone else for supplying our "small stuff." When we leave God out of the loop, we are guilty of giving God's glory to someone else. Let God be Lord of your life, your entire life, and you will have peace. An African Proverb reads: "A heavy burden does not kill on the day it is carried." Jesus says why carry them large or small? Cast all of your cares, large and small, upon Him because He cares for you!

Reflection Questions:

What small things do you need to trust the Lord to do for you? What are the big things you need to trust the Lord to do for you?

_____

_____

_____

Prayer:

Lord you are the God of all creation. You are the Creator of all things, large and small. Help me remember that I can lean on your wisdom for things large and small in my life. Give me wisdom. Show me how to lean on you, knowing that when I trust you, you will direct my paths. Direct my paths today and every day.

The Power

Rev. April Van Rader

Scripture:

But you will receive power when the Holy Spirit has come upon you; and you will be my witnesses in Jerusalem, in all Judea and Samaria, and to the ends of the earth." Acts1:8 NRSV

Reflection:

Before Peter and the other disciples were baptized in the Holy Spirit, they were just a band of weak and fearful men. They were so afraid that they were in hiding after Jesus was arrested; after Jesus was taken away they fled and locked themselves behind closed doors. Peter was so fearful that he denied ever knowing Christ, but after he was baptized in the Holy Spirit (Acts 5:5) Peter had such an anointing that people would wait for him to walk by so that they would be healed by being in the darkness of his shadow. After Peter was anointed with the power of the Holy Spirit he became fearless; he was threatened, beaten, imprisoned, exiled and tortured, yet he never stopped preaching about The Lord.

Let's look at some famous quotes that Peter himself could have penned: "*The past is a place of reference, not a place of* residence."[2] Peter could have had this to say about his situation when the Holy Spirit had come upon him: "*Courage is fear that has said its prayers.*"[3] Peter was sure about his future because Jesus left him with these parting words: (Matthew 28:20) "*For surely I am with you always even to the end of the age.*" It is true that a person cannot be touched by the power of God and not be changed.

Reflection Questions:

What is the one thing about yourself that you would like to see changed after encounter with God's Holy Spirit? Ask God to touch this thing with the power of the Holy Spirit. To whom can you witness today because you have been touched with the power of God?

_____

_____

_____

_____

_____

_____

_____

_____

_____

_____

_____

_____

_____

_____

_____

_____

_____

_____

_____

---

[2] Willie Jolley, *A Setback Is a Setup for a Comeback* (New York: Saint Martin's Press, 1999).

[3] Joyce Meyer, *I Dare You: Embrace Life with Passion* (New York: Faith Words, 2007).

67

Prayer:

Dear God, so many hurtful things have happened in my life I feel powerless. Sometimes, like Peter, I deny that I know you. As much as I want to leave my past behind, I don't seem to be able to get away from these memories. Help me remember always that who I am is not defined by where I've been, but by where I am going. Heal my memories, heal my woundedness. Help me remember that you are always with me. Help me live by your power in me. Touch me. Change me. Let me be a blessing because of your touch and my testimony be a blessing to someone today.

The Boat

Rev. April Van Rader

Scripture:

And early in the morning he came walking toward them on the sea. But when the disciples saw him walking on the sea, they were terrified, saying, "It is a ghost!" And they cried out in fear. But immediately Jesus spoke to them and said, "Take heart, it is I; do not be afraid." Peter answered him, "Lord, if it is you, command me to come to you on the water." He said, "Come." Matthew 14:25-29 NRSV

Reflection:

We often make it a point to place emphasis on the fact that Peter took his eyes off Jesus and began to sink. It's human nature to point out the weaknesses of others in an effort to justify ourselves and to make ourselves look greater in the eyes of our audience. Why not give credit to Peter for having greater faith than the rest? It must have taken tremendous courage to step out of the boat into the darkness of the sea! Peter knew that Jesus was capable of walking on the water, but could he, a mere man, a wretched sinner, do the same? It took the faith that believes that through Jesus Christ we can accomplish more and become more than we ever thought possible.

We too can step out into the darkness of the unknown in full confidence that as long as we keep our eyes on Jesus we won't sink. Once we fix our eyes on Jesus and not the raging waters below we will begin to walk above our circumstances. Jesus bids us to come out of the boat so that we may come to realize that Jesus, not the boat, is our security. The boat of our lives may be sinking, but Jesus is telling us that our only hope and safety is with him. We just need to activate our mustard seed of faith and step out onto the water, trusting that Jesus will be there to lead and guide every step of the way!

Reflection Question:

If you knew that you wouldn't sink, what steps of faith would you be willing to take out of the boat? Ask God to help you take those steps today!

_____
_____
_____
_____
_____
_____
_____

Prayer:

Dear God, it is so dark and the water is so deep. I hear you calling me. I feel you calling me. I want to come. I want to come to you. Yet, I am afraid—afraid of the darkness, afraid of the water. Remind me that even in the midst of the darkness of my life, you are still the Light of the World. Give me courage to step out of the boat today.

Martha, Can You Hear Me Now?

Rev. April Van Rader

Scripture:

Now as they went on their way, he entered a certain village, where a woman named Martha welcomed him into her home. She had a sister named Mary, who sat at the Lord's feet and listened to what he was saying. But Martha was distracted by her many tasks; so she came to him and asked, "Lord, do you not care that my sister has left me to do all the work by myself? Tell her then to help me." But the Lord answered her, "Martha, Martha, you are worried and distracted by many things; there is need of only one thing. Mary has chosen the better part, which will not be taken away from her." Luke 10:38-41 NRSV

Reflection:

Martha, relax, chill . . . I'm trying to tell you something. Hear me. I'm coming to your home not for you to feed me, but to feed you! Martha didn't understand that she didn't have to prepare a meal; Jesus was already feeding the guests. We are so much like Martha. We are like Martha because with all of our *busy-ness* we don't take the time to hear what God is saying to us. We are so intent upon pleasing people that we fail to please God; we neglect our first love. The Divine Order of things is: God first in all things. When we truly put God first, family, work, church, and all the other parts of our lives will fall into place. When we become so busy that our priorities are misplaced we need to stop and slow down so that we can hear what Jesus is saying to us: "Relax, chill, I'm trying to tell you something."

Reflection Questions:

What are the things in your life that make you too busy to hear God? How will you rearrange your life so that you can hear God?

_____

_____

_____

_____

_____

_____

_____

_____

_____

_____

_____

_____

_____

_____

_____

_____

Prayer:

Dear God, my life is so full. I am grateful for it all—home, work, church, school, and community. Yet, it seems I always have too much to do and too little time to get it done. Too often, I find I neglect my time with you and your Word. Forgive me, Lord, for putting you last when I should put you first. Help me get and keep my priorities straight. Help me remember that when I put you first, all things will be added to me.

Love Your Neighbor

Rev. April Van Rader

Scripture:

For the commandments against adultery and murder and stealing and coveting -- and any other commandment -- are all summed up in this one commandment: "Love your neighbor as yourself." Romans 13:9 NLT

Reflection:

Scripture says that our love should extend beyond our fence, beyond our churches, beyond our beloved country and out into the entire world. Jesus came to admit all into the kingdom, including all who were thought to be outcasts, rejects, lepers, sinners, unaccepted, lowly, poor, needy, unloved and unwanted.

Loving one's neighbor means denying yourself, putting our neighbor's concerns before our own, esteeming our neighbor more highly than ourselves. Loving our neighbors means honoring and respecting the humanity in every person-- period. Any time we devalue the humanity of anyone, for any reason, we have failed to live by this basic ethical principle of the Christian faith. Our neighbor is the world; we are all on this planet together and we must do our part in order to maintain good relationships among all.

Loving one's neighbor doesn't just happen. It requires intentional effort to engage the world, starting with those closest to us and extending to all. Whether we realize it or not, whatever we send out, good or bad, will always comes back to us. Let us send out good expecting that good will come back to us.

Reflection Questions:

How many times today have you neglected to reach out to someone who was different from yourself? Why did you devalue this person? Ask God to heal the woundedness inside you that caused you not to love your neighbor. Having examined yourself and taken this log out of your eye, to whom can you reach out in the spirit of love and inclusiveness today?

_____
_____
_____
_____
_____
_____
_____

Prayer:

Lord, please forgive me. Too often, more than I would like to admit, I have turned away from and neglected my neighbor. I have looked the other way when I could have helped. I have been silent when my words could have made a difference. I have forgotten people I should have remembered. I have overlooked people I should have paid attention to. Forgive me Lord. Teach me. Show me how to love my neighbor as I love myself.

The Light Has Come

Rev. April Van Rader

Scripture:

And God said, "Let there be light," and there was light. Genesis 1:3: NIV

Reflection:

The earth was formless, empty and dark, but nonetheless, God's Spirit **hovered over it!**

What a perfect description of us before we accept Jesus Christ as our Lord and Savior. B*efore we are born again, we* don't have a **form**, A PURPOSE, and we're EMPTY. But **God hovers over us,** waiting for us to come to him, so that he can fill our empty space with His Spirit. *Oh,* the DARKNESS, the sin, the disgrace, guilt, fear, restlessness; the shame of the things we've done. How dark it all is! God's goal is to transform us. Rather than the light of God exposing all our shameful sin for the whole world to see, God illuminates us from the inside out and, surprisingly enough, **we** expose Satan and the hold he had on us by the telling others what God has done for us, by giving our testimony!

We can use the creation story as a metaphor for the creation that is still taking place today as each person who comes to know God through the redemption of Jesus Christ is created anew. In the Gospel of John, creation didn't happen without

Jesus Christ and without Jesus Christ our new creation cannot take place. God's Spirit in us will give our life PURPOSE and MEANING. We will understand that the **emptiness** we felt was a longing for the presence of God. Before the Holy Spirit came to dwell with us, we were living in **darkness** longing for God to light our path so that we could find our way, find our purpose. Praise be to God for being the light unto our path!

Reflection Question:

What darkness in you has the light of God revealed?

_____
_____
_____
_____
_____
_____
_____

Prayer:

Light of the World, I need you in my life today. When I read the newspapers, when I turn on the television and radio, when I check out the Internet, it reminds me that much is amiss in the world. When I think about my life, I realize that much is amiss in my world, too. If I am honest with myself, and with you, I must admit that there are times when I too feel formless and empty, in the midst of the darkness around me, in the midst of the darkness within me. Light my path. Help me find my purpose. Help me live the abundant life, the life you came to give me.

A Quiet Spirit

Rev. April Van Rader

Scripture:

"But I have stilled and quieted my soul; like a weaned child with its mother, like a weaned child is my soul within me." Psalm 131:2 *NIV*

Reflection:

The greatest lesson that David learned from his encounters with God was how to listen for God's voice. God has a quiet way of speaking to us, and it's only when we are calm enough to hear with our *spiritual ears* that we will truly hear from him. David heard God speak in the midst of some of the greatest trials and tribulations in his life, including Saul's threats on his life and his adultery with Bathsheba.

Like David, you and I can hear God speak when our reception is at its best, when we are still and quiet before God. However, getting to a quiet place is not always easy. When the problems of life are screaming our name, when situations are knocking at our door, this is the time when we need the peace that Jesus promised—the peace that surpasses our understanding. As much as we need God's peace, these are often the times when we are least likely to seek it.

In times like these we need the peace that reminds us to say "I understand that I have problems right now, but God has promised me peace." We need the peace that reminds us to say "I believe what God's Word says. It says that I don't have to concern myself with things that are too great for me" and to confess, "When it's all said and done, God will carry me through this situation, because He knows what's best for me." What we must remember is that God will keep His promises to us; we need to be still so that we can hear His voice again.

Reflection Questions:

Have you experienced the power of God's peace to reduce the stress in your life? Do you take time daily to find God's quiet place?

_____
_____
_____
_____
_____
_____
_____

Prayer:

God of Peace, my world is so full of noise. How can I possibly get my bearings, how can I possibly hold the pieces of my life together when there are so many demands—spouse, children, friends, work, church, school, community? I need you Lord. I need the quiet place that only you can give. Help me find a way to take time to spend alone with you every day. I know the quality of my life will be much better for it. Thank you for every quiet moment in your presence. What a blessing these moments are in my life.

Firewalls in Our Lives

Rev. Dr. Jacquetta Chambers

Scripture:

Therefore take up the whole armor of God, so that you may be able to withstand on that evil day, and having done everything, to stand firm. Stand therefore, and fasten the belt of truth around your waist, and put on the breastplate of righteousness. As shoes for your feet put on whatever will make you ready to proclaim the gospel of peace. With all of these, take the shield of faith, with which you will be able to quench all the flaming arrows of the evil one. Take the helmet of salvation, and the sword of the Spirit, which is the word of God. Pray in the Spirit at all times in every prayer and supplication. To that end keep alert and always persevere in supplication for all the saints. Ephesians 6:10-18 NRSV

Reflection:

The events of the September 11 (9/11) tragedy proved our nation was not adequately protected. Troops were stationed in places we expected attacks, but we were not prepared for the attack on our families in airplanes.

In computing, a firewall has been defined as "a security system consisting of a combination of hardware and software that limits the exposure of a computer or network to attack." These attacks can cause a computer to get stuck, hang, i.e. crash. When that happens it's easy to lose important data. We know when we fail to update our computer firewalls we are vulnerable to all sorts of crashes and viruses. Clean-up can be a real chore. Would we not have been better off just to bite the bullet and buy the necessary software so we can protect our hardware? "

Sometimes this rings true of God's people. The forces of despair, depression, disappointment and deceit are many times stronger that we ever imagine. Having good firewall protection means arming ourselves with the spiritual resources of God's security system. We need both armor (hardware) and prayer (software) that defeats Satan's attacks. We know that everyday life has a multitude of "issues, problems, and challenges" Why not stay spiritually ready to meet them?

Reflection Questions:

What forces are difficult for you to defeat? What firewalls of faith do you use to protect you from defeat?

_____
_____
_____
_____
_____
_____
_____

Prayer:

Dear God, I know I need your protection for living. You have already provided every spiritual blessing that heaven has to offer. Forgive me for not using what you have already given. Help me keep my spiritual firewalls updated and current.

Which is More Desired: Blessings or Riches?

Rev. Dr. Jacquetta Chambers

Scripture:

The faithful will abound with blessings, but one who is in a hurry to be rich will not go unpunished. Proverbs 28:20 NRSV

Reflection:

Patti LaBelle, a well-known vocal artist published a book called, *Don't Block Your Blessings.* In the book she talks of the many ways she blocked her own blessings, and how we block ours. Blessings in many ways are taken for granted and aligned with whatever we accomplish with our intellect, will and might. What about the blessings of and from God that have nothing to do with our accomplishments? What about the blessings of health, strength and a clear mind that only God can give?

Unfortunately, we confuse who we are with what we have (or don't have). Our desire for material riches clouds the view of spiritual blessings we already have. Constantly striving to get more "stuff" feeds into the secular assessment of our worth and wealth.

Yet, this scripture in Proverbs tells us that being FAITHFUL is the key to blessings. This proverb comes with a warning that anyone who attempts to get rich quickly, i.e. by using deceitful and dishonest means, will <u>not</u> go unpunished. The scripture makes it plain: riches earned by dishonest means come with problems galore. Life has enough problems as it is. Why add to them with ill-gotten gain?

Our blessings are blocked when our DESIRES do not line up with the Word of God. We need to ask ourselves: What do we desire most? Where does our fulfillment lie? Are we more concerned with being blessed by God, or being rich by the world's standards?

Reflection Question:

What do you desire most—blessings or riches?

_____
_____
_____
_____

Prayer:

Dear God, we live in a consumer-driven materialistic culture. The media constantly bombard us with messages that encourage us to spend money that we don't have for things we don't need. Deep down, I know I should resist this temptation. I want to keep up with the newest, the latest, and the greatest—often to my own detriment. Help me seek your blessings instead of the world's riches.

Everyday Low Prices

Rev. Dr. Jacquetta Chambers

Scripture:

Wait and listen, everyone who is thirsty! Come to the waters; and he who has no money, come, buy and eat! Yes, come, buy [priceless, spiritual] wine and milk without money and without price [simply for the self-surrender that accepts the blessing]. Isaiah 55:1-3 Amplified Bible

Reflection:

WAL-MART advertises "Everyday Low Prices." Wal-Mart does not have to have seasonal sales, or drastic price deductions to circumvent its competitors, it already has the lowest prices. The consumer does not need to shop around or look for better bargains or better quality. What a claim!! No one else can make a claim like this except Christ Jesus. For just 30 pieces of silver (a rock bottom bargain price) Christ was sold as the sacrifice for our transgressions.

In Isaiah 55:1 the righteous are invited to acquire water, food, wine and milk without giving anything in exchange. This low price is synonymous with what we call "FREE." Skeptics believe everything has a price. From their perspective this particular message requires a "price"—some action on the part of the receiver, i.e. to open their ears, come to the Lord, and hear what God has to say. Yet, if and when we take verse on its own merit, what God offers is FREE. The verses in

Isaiah mirror Wal-Mart's slogan, "Everyday Low Prices." It is an everyday low price to come, to listen, and be attentive with open ears to God's leading and guiding.

Reflection Question:

God's arms are open wide giving us what we need for life. Are you willing to embrace him, listen, and be attentive to what God has to say?

_____
_____
_____
_____
_____
_____
_____
_____
_____
_____
_____
_____
_____
_____
_____
_____
_____
_____
_____
_____

Prayer:

Dear God, what you give, you give freely from your heart. In the same spirit help me receive what you have so generously given.

Please, Don't Make Me Take It Back!

Rev. Dr. Jacquetta Chambers

Scripture:

Nathan said to the king, "Go, do all that you have in mind; for the LORD is with you." 2 Samuel 7:3 NRSV

Reflection:

As I reflect on this verse, I'm reminded of a story about a teacher once told a student who acted out continuously that he would never amount to anything good. The student was in the 5th grade. This would be a crushing blow to anyone.

Although, the student failed the 5th grade, that summer he lost one of his friends to gang violence. That was the turning point for him. He graduated with honors and went on to be a noteworthy teacher himself. Later in life when the teacher saw him again, she had to take it back. What she thought was not God's plan for his life. God had a better plan than she could ever imagine.

In the Bible, Nathan, like the teacher, had to backtrack on what he said. King David wanted to build a house for God. He could not be at peace with himself or his own way of living, knowing that God did not have a residence. He set his mind to it and told the prophet Nathan about his plans. Nathan, believing this surely was a good thing, told David, to go ahead and do it.

That night, God instructed Nathan to go and tell David something totally different. In other words, Nathan spoke too soon. He equated his thoughts with God's. God said no such thing. God instructed Nathan to go to David and take back what Nathan had said. Can you imagine how Nathan, a man of God, must have felt like? Can you imagine him awakening that morning, and dreading the task of telling David that he would not build God's house, but that his son (Solomon) would do so? Sometimes we too have to take back some of the things we have said. Often, we put ourselves in situations where we speak too soon. Without understanding, we judge falsely. If we are to do what is right, like the teacher, like Nathan we know we have to take it back.

Reflection Questions:

What things have you said, that you had to take back? How did you feel?

_____
_____
_____
_____
_____
_____
_____
_____
_____
_____
_____
_____

_____

_____

_____

_____

_____

_____

_____

_____

_____

_____

_____

_____

_____

_____

_____

_____

_____

_____

_____

_____

_____

_____

_____

_____

Prayer:

Dear God, sometimes my mouth gets me into trouble. Sometimes I put my foot in my mouth and speak before I think. Too often, I ignore your prompting me to keep silent. Then I regret what I've said and try to smooth things over without having to apologize and correct what I mistakenly said. Forgive me, Lord. Help me control my tongue so I won't have to take it back. When I do need to take it back, help me swallow my pride and do the right thing.

What Have We Done?

Rev. Dr. Jacquetta Chambers

Scripture:

And being warned of God in a dream that they should not return to Herod, they departed into their own country another route. Matthew 2:12 NIV.

Reflection:

When the Christmas Story is told each year, the Wise Men are a central part of the narrative. Although the scripture does not say there were just 3 wise men, we line our mangers with them. The gifts they brought to the house for the Christ child have been etched in our memories. Yet, there is another part of the story that needs to be remembered.

Herod asked the wise men to bring him word when they had found the child. They were warned in a dream not to go back to Herod, so they went another way. Feeling that he had been mocked by the wise men, Herod had all of the male children in Bethlehem two years and under, killed. "In Rama there was heard lamentations, weeping and great mourning."

It would seem that with every cry from a mother whose child Herod had killed, the wise men would ask themselves "What have we done?" As children died around them, surely, they asked themselves that question. The guilt and confusion of doing what they had been told impacting death all around them had to be a tremendous weight on their shoulders.

This story reminds us that following God's directions does not mean we will understand what happens around us. We may not even understand or agree with the fallout from our following. Nonetheless, our call is to follow. Today we surely must have heartfelt empathy and sympathy for the wise men for what must have been a very difficult situation.

Reflection Question:

When have you followed God's directions, only to ask, "What have I done?"

_____
_____
_____
_____
_____
_____
_____
_____
_____
_____
_____
_____
_____
_____
_____
_____
_____
_____
_____
_____
_____
_____

_____
_____
_____
_____
_____
_____
_____
_____
_____
_____
_____
_____
_____
_____
_____
_____
_____
_____
_____
_____
_____
_____
_____

Prayer:

Dear God, I know you never promised me a bed of roses, but sometimes it seems there are too many unforeseen thorns along the path of faith. Many people think that following you means that all of life will be wonderful. It's hard to come to terms with the notion that roses, and thorns are inseparable. These thorns sometimes have a negative effect in my life and the lives of others. Lord, help me accept the reality that there may be negative fallout when I choose to follow you. Let me be faithful to the life and the tasks to which you are calling me—even if there are thorns along the way.

Fresh Bread

Rev. Denise Blakely

Scripture:

*I am the bread of life. Your ancestors ate manna in the
wilderness, and they died. This is the bread that comes
down from heaven, so that one may eat of it and not die.
John 6:48-50 NRSV*

Reflection:

We all have to eat. Nourishment is a requirement for every
living thing on the earth. Not only do we all need
sustenance, we need it every day. However, we must take
care that what we put into our bodies is wholesome and
beneficial to our health and wellbeing. We know that old,
stale food will not serve our nutritional needs but may make
us very, very ill.

It is the same with our thoughts and actions. Just as physical
malnutrition stunts physical growth, spiritual malnutrition will
stunt and distort potential maturity and growth of mind and
spirit. Living on a diet of past hurts and indignations will
result in spiritual malnourishment for the believer. Spiritual
malnutrition will result in misplaced anger and an inability to
cope with current problems. We have to take care that the
bread of the past is not the bread of the present. We have

Jesus, the living, fresh bread in our lives as the catalyst for new thinking, new actions, and new joy.

Reflection Questions:

What is in your spiritual diet? Are you dwelling on a past that is gone or are you greeting each new day as a new beginning? What do you have to give up so you can embrace your present and look forward to your future?

_____

_____

_____

_____

_____

_____

_____

_____

_____

_____

_____

_____

_____

Prayer:

Lord, I know I need to lose some weight, and not just physical weight. I need to lose some emotional weight. I am weary of the weight of anger, hurt, and disappointment that I've been carrying around much too long. Bread of Heaven, your ways are not my ways, your thoughts are not my thoughts. Feed me with your thoughts and ways. May your words be my words, your perspective my perspective on life. Let me be malnourished no more.

Walk in Power

Rev. Denise Blakely

Scripture:

Finally, be strong in the Lord and in the strength of his power. Ephesians 6:10 NRSV

Reflection:

Life is like running a marathon and sometimes the reward for work is more work. It would be wonderful if there were an endless supply of strength that we could tap into to keep going.

The challenge of daily living calls us to continually meet every deadline, complete every task, and climb every mountain. Solve a crisis for breakfast, finish all chores for lunch, have warm fuzzy hugs for loved ones exactly when they need them for dinner, and for dessert, plan more work for the next day. Is it any wonder that we are constantly pulled, perplexed and just plain pooped!!!

How wonderful it is to know that we have access to an eternal source of wisdom, direction and power. The strength we need is ours for the asking—no strings attached, no dotted line to sign. Whenever and wherever we are overwhelmed, pull over, pull away, get to a quiet place and ask God for help. All our tasks and burdens in this life could use a second pair of hands for help. How much easier these tasks become when the same hands that created the universe intervene on our behalf.

Reflection Questions:

Why is it so hard to ask for help? What aspects of life could you use some help, right now? What do you need God's help with? Who else do you need to ask for help today?

_____
_____
_____
_____
_____
_____
_____
_____
_____
_____
_____
_____
_____
_____
_____
_____
_____

Prayer:

Awesome Lord, I know my help comes from you. Yet, sometimes like a small child, I find myself, before I realize it, trying to do it all by myself. Forgive me, Lord. Too often I consult you last—after I've tried everything else I can think of—instead of first. Forgive me, Lord. May your Holy Spirit be my Helper—today and always. Give me wisdom and strength to ask for and receive help from my sisters and my brothers when I need it.

Details, Details, Details

Rev. Denise Blakely

Scripture:

Who are you to pass judgment on servants of another? It is before their own lord that they stand or fall. And they will be upheld, for the Lord is able to make them stand. Romans 14:4 NRSV

Reflection:

Sometimes the devil is really in the details. Granted, there are some amazing and crazy things going on in this world and in some of our lives also. It is only natural to try and maintain control over the events and circumstances that come our way. Problems arise, however, when we try to exercise that same control over the lives of other people. Each one of us has a set of circumstances, behaviors, beliefs, habits, thoughts, and motivations that make us unique. Only God knows everything about people and their situation. That is why we have to be careful concerning any advice we might give.

Let us not miss the work and direction that God has for our own lives because we are paying too much attention to the details in the lives of others. Prayer is the most powerful thing we can do for anyone. Let us pray for one another and put the details in God's hands where they belong.

Reflection Question:

Who do you need to pray for and leave the details to God?

_____
_____
_____
_____
_____
_____
_____
_____
_____
_____
_____
_____
_____
_____
_____

Prayer:

Dear God, sometimes I take on too much responsibility for the lives of others, especially family and friends who are close to me. I want the best for them. Too often I say and do things I shouldn't trying to do what I think is best. Forgive me, Lord. Help me hold my tongue and allow me to help only when and how you think I should. Lord, I pray for fulfillment of your purpose in the lives of _____ (names of the persons you're praying for). Free me of trying to control their lives. Free me to love them according to your will and your way. Help me trust you enough to leave the details of their lives to you.

Everlasting Hope

Rev. Denise Blakely

Scripture:

For there is hope for a tree, if it is cut down, that it will sprout again, and that its shoots will not cease. Job 14:7 NRSV

Reflection:

The cultivation of forests is a very precise science that is not for the faint of heart. There are so many factors that impact upon the growth of trees. Drought, floods, infestation are but a few of the challenges faced by those who are the caretakers of our forests. Lighting and the fires caused by careless campers, a tossed cigarette, or arson, results in the destruction of thousands upon thousands of acres of trees, scorched land, destroyed homes and the loss of life.

In the midst of all this destruction, new trees are born on top of the ashes of destruction. Some of the most breathtaking, dense, beautiful forests were created in the midst of devastation and barren, burnt land.

We have the same reassurance from God that new life is still manifesting in nature and in our lives every moment of every day. Out of brokenness and disappointment, God is constantly rebuilding our lives, individually and collectively. If we are willing to hold onto hope for better days, in the midst of turmoil, new strength, new direction, and new life will spring forth from the ashes in our lives.

Reflection Questions:

Is there a need for renewal in your life? Are you afraid to ask God to create something new in your life? Why?

_____
_____
_____
_____
_____
_____
_____
_____
_____
_____
_____
_____
_____
_____
_____
_____
_____
_____
_____
_____
_____

Prayer:

God of all creation, you know how to make all things new. I come before you today in need of your renewal, in need of your healing for my brokenness. May your new life spring forth in my life today.

Forever, Praise!

Rev. Denise Blakely

Scripture:

So even to old age and grey hairs, O God, do not forsake me, until I proclaim your might to all the generations to come, Psalms 71:18 NRSV

Reflection:

God's Infinite power is available to us at every stage of life. The grace that is with us from the moment of conception is the grace that accompanies us from birth to death. We can call upon the Lord in any situation and lean on the Everlasting Presence of God. Because of this access to God's power, we accumulate a lifetime of wisdom and testimonies of all the moments that we were touched by God. All those times that the Lord intervened on our behalf to uplift, heal, strengthen and direct us for our benefit are lessons learned that we can pass on to others.

There is no age restriction on praise! When we tell the story of God's work in our lives, we are praising God for all the mighty works that we have witnessed. In other words, our praise has gone beyond just what we believe with our mind. Praise rooted in our hearts because of what we have experienced, because of what we know is true! Since we know that our joy begins and ends with God, we should be willing to proclaim the goodness and power of God, not only among our peers, but also to those who come behind us.

Reflection Question:

Is there someone who could benefit from your story, your unique praise and testimony?

_____
_____
_____
_____
_____
_____
_____
_____
_____
_____
_____
_____
_____
_____
_____
_____
_____
_____
_____
_____
_____

Prayer:

God of Eternal Blessing, help me remember that I am blessed to be a blessing. Help me remember that you did not bless me to keep the news of your goodness to myself. Heal me. Make me whole so that I can share my story with those who need to hear it. Show me whom I might bless by sharing my story today.

Don't Let Anything Stand in the Way!

Rev. Dr. Alfie Wines

Scripture:

Then Jesus told his disciples a parable to show them that they should always pray and not give up. Luke 18:1 NIV

Reflection:

As beneficial as prayer is to our lives, we often miss the blessings because it seems that something always gets in the way. Distractions are endless--phone calls, people, responsibilities at home, at work, and in the community. Why is it that so often, despite our best intentions, it seems that something always gets in the way?

We must face and deal with whatever hinders us. From a theological view, we must wrestle with our understanding of God. We will not pray unless we believe that: 1) God exists, 2) God is good, and 3) God is responsive to our prayers. From a practical view, we must intentionally reorder our lives if we are to spend time with God and with God's Word. Neither of these is an easy task. Yet, if we make the effort, God will bless it. If we persevere, we will find that our time with God and with God's Word is *more* than worth the effort.

If we fall short, there's no need to be hard on ourselves. This is one time when we need to keep trying 'til we get it right. We must refuse to give up. Decide now that you won't let anyone, or anything stand in your way as you seek the face of God.

Reflection Questions:

What are some of your hindrances to maintaining a consistent prayer life? What can you do to overcome them?

_____

_____

_____

_____

_____

_____

_____

_____

_____

_____

_____

_____

_____

_____

_____

_____

Prayer:

Why, God, why? Why is it that I am so easily distracted from a life of prayer? I want to pray. I know I should pray. Yet, somehow, I fall prey to, give in to the temptation not to pray. I know that weakens me for the business of living. I know Jesus was a man of prayer. I know he set the example of the power of prayer. He prayed constantly, about everything—alone and in the presence of others. I know there is no substitute for prayer in the life of the believer. Help me, Lord! Help me! Help me say my prayers so I can stay connected to you.

Thank You, Lord, For Being There

Rev. Dr. Alfie Wines

Scripture:

He who keeps you will not slumber. Behold, He who keeps Israel will neither slumber nor sleep. Psalm 121: 3b,4 NASB

Reflection:

Through good times and bad, we can thank God, just for being there. Who else but God can we count on to always be there, 24 hours a day, 7 days a week (24-7). Late at night and early in the morning, we can count on God to always be there for us.

Aren't you glad that God never sleeps, never slumbers. How else could we talk to you at two or three in the morning. . . in the stillness of the night . . . In the quiet of the morning?

In the stillness, in the quiet, we can hear ourselves think. We can hear from and tune in to God's ever abiding presence.

Reflection Question:

What has God done in your life that you appreciate the most? Take time to thank God for all He has done for you.

_____

_____

_____

_____

_____

_____
_____
_____
_____
_____
_____
_____
_____
_____
_____
_____
_____
_____
_____
_____
_____
_____
_____
_____
_____
_____
_____
_____
_____
_____
_____
_____
_____

Prayer:

Life is so complex and there are so many things to think about.   I'm glad that no matter what the problem, the place to begin is with You. Thank you, Lord, for being there. I can always count on you!

So Much to Pray About

Rev. Dr. Alfie Wines

Scripture:

The steps of the godly are directed by the LORD. He delights in every detail of their lives." Psalm 37:23 NLT

Reflection:

God's Word says we should pray about everything. Everything? Sometimes I think, "O God, there's so much to pray about!!"

But, it is wonderful to know that God cares about the details of our lives. No need to try to figure out what is or is not appropriate to talk to God about. A reading of the Psalms makes it clear. David and the other Psalmists prayed about everything!! Friends, enemies, in good times and bad . . . they told God everything—even when everything included ill wishes for their enemies—and looked forward to God's answer.

Reflection Questions:

What are some of the big things that you pray about? What are some of the little things that you pray about? Take time to thank God for caring about both the big and little things in your life.

_____

_____

_____

_____

_____
_____
_____
_____
_____
_____
_____
_____
_____
_____
_____
_____
_____
_____
_____
_____
_____
_____
_____
_____
_____
_____
_____
_____
_____

Prayer:

Lord, when I ask, "Everything?" your answer is a resounding YES--big things, little things, all things--EVERYTHING!! I thank you Lord for your resounding "Yes, everything," Lord, because on days like today, I *need* to pray!!

But, I Don't Feel Like Praying!

Rev. Dr. Alfie Wines

Scripture:

Never stop praying. 1 Thessalonians 5:17 God's Word

Reflection:

As Christians, we know the importance of prayer. We know that we should "pray without ceasing." Yet, sometimes, if the truth be told, sometimes, we just don't feel like praying. Sometimes, we're busy and don't want to take time to pray. Sometimes, we're ill and don't want to pray. Sometimes we're mad at God and don't want to pray. Sometimes, we're tired of praying about the same thing, over and over. Sometimes, it seems God is distant, does not hear, does not care, or is slow to answer.

Pray anyway. Pray short prayers. Pray long prayers. Just pray so you can keep in touch with God. Yes, even if it seems God is distant, does not hear, does not care, or is slow to answer— pray anyway!

Reflection Questions:

Describe a time in your life when you didn't feel like praying. What was going on? Were you afraid to pray about what was going on? Did you find God faithful, even when you didn't pray? Take time to thank God for His faithfulness and for loving you--even when you didn't feel like praying.

_____
_____
_____
_____
_____
_____
_____
_____
_____
_____
_____
_____
_____
_____
_____
_____
_____
_____
_____
_____
_____
_____
_____

Prayer:

Dear God, I must confess. Sometimes I find it hard, very hard to pray. I am torn. I want to pray. I need to pray, but somebody or something gets in the way. Life hurts and disappoints me. I know I shouldn't, but I sometimes get angry with you because you don't seem to care about me. Yet, I know that your Word makes it clear that you do hear, and you do care. So, Lord, help me separate my foolish feelings from the truth of your Word. Help me pray, even when I don't feel like praying!

Convicted, Corrected, But Never Condemned

Rev. Dr. Alfie Wines

Scripture:

No condemnation now hangs over the head of those who are 'in' Christ Jesus. For the new spiritual principle of life 'in' Christ Jesus lifts me out of the old vicious circle of sin and death. Romans 8:1,2 PHILLIPS

Reflection:

It is to our detriment that we confuse conviction with condemnation. In the confusion, we get stuck. We linger and anguish in our guilt for days, weeks, months, or sometimes, even years. Thanks be to God who can work even this agony to our good!

We miss so much of the enjoyment and so many of the good things in life as we try to pay for and punish ourselves despite the fact that Christ paid the penalty 2,000 years ago, a penalty that God designed even before the beginning of creation. What foolish creatures we are!!

If we learn the difference between conviction, correction, and condemnation, we can be free to confess and move forward in our lives. For, while we may not like it, we can live with being convicted and corrected. It is the condemnation that we cannot live with. It is when we expect more than God expects, it is when we try to become our own god that we feel the need to condemn ourselves. In our desire to be our best and because of our guilt, we often go far beyond any conviction and correction that God bestows.

Aren't you glad that we don't have to be burdened by negative emotions that result from our sins? Aren't you glad that in reality when we sin, because of Jesus, sin no longer has dominion over us? We have learned an important lesson in life when we learn to accept God's conviction and correction gracefully. Aren't you grateful that because of Jesus, there is no condemnation for sin? Not now, not ever!!

Reflection Questions:

Do you recall a time when you felt convicted, corrected, condemned about something amiss in your life? Take time to thank God for convicting and correcting you. Take time to thank God that because of Jesus you are never condemned for anything amiss in your life.

_____
_____
_____
_____
_____
_____
_____
_____
_____
_____
_____
_____
_____
_____
_____
_____
_____

_____
_____
_____
_____
_____
_____
_____
_____
_____
_____
_____
_____
_____
_____
_____
_____
_____
_____
_____
_____
_____
_____
_____
_____

Prayer:

Thank you Lord! Hallelujah! I am so glad that no matter what, because of the blood of

Jesus, I am not condemned. When I feel bowed down in guilt and regret, remind me Lord that Jesus died for me. He came to give me abundant life and I don't have to live in the shadows of yesterday. Instead, I can embrace the sunshine of today and tomorrow.

Closer Than We Think

Rev. Dr. Alfie Wines

Scripture:

The king will answer them "I can guarantee this truth: Whatever you did for one of my brothers or sisters, no matter how unimportant they seemed, you did for me." Matthew 25:40 God's Word

Reflection:

Is it really true that even when we didn't notice God's Presence, God has always been with us on our journey? Is it really true that God is closer to us than we are to ourselves? Could it be that God is so close we sometimes overlook God?

Sometimes seeking God reminds me of trying to find a tiny, clear, contact lens. The fact that they are tiny and clear makes them hard to find. That's because they take on the appearance of whatever it falls on. Could it be that God's Sprit is so close to us, so deep in us that we fail to see God? Could it be that we miss seeing God in ourselves and in others? After all Jesus said that whether good or ill, when we've done it to the least of these, you've done it unto him. The spiritual truth is that God's spirit is always present, drawing us closer to God. Our prayer should be, "Lord, help us become more tuned in, more aware of your presence in ourselves and in others as we live each day.

Reflection Question:

Can you recall a time when you overlooked God's presence in yourself and others missing opportunities to experience and share God's love in the world? Take time to make your confession and talk with God about it.

_____
_____
_____
_____
_____
_____
_____
_____
_____
_____
_____
_____
_____
_____
_____
_____
_____
_____

Prayer:

Lord, forgive me for the times when I overlooked your presence in others and myself. I know that each time I overlook your presence in anyone I miss an opportunity to experience and share the flow of your love in the world. I want to experience the flow of your love more each day. Help me look through your lens for looking through your lens gives me the proper perspective on life.

God's Perspective

Rev. Dr. Alfie Wines

(Dedicated to Mrs. Jean Thomas

at Campus Drive United Methodist Community Church)

Scripture:

For my thoughts are not your thoughts, nor are your ways my ways, says the LORD. For as the heavens are higher than the earth, so are my ways higher than your ways and my thoughts than your thoughts. Isaiah 55:8-9 NRSV

Reflection:

If only we could learn to see ourselves and our problems from God's perspective. Imagine the toughest problem that you are dealing with right now. Think of it from close up. Feel the tension, the stress that it causes you. Now imagine you are among the tree tops looking down on your situation. How does it feel to have put some distance between you and the problem—even if only for a moment.

Now imagine you are sitting in the window seat of an airplane and that the problem is a point somewhere on the ground beneath you. Think about your problem again—same problem, same issues, same people, same circumstances— yet the whole thing seems smaller, doesn't it? Continue looking at your problem from further and further away—into our galaxy, into the universe, from the place where light begins. Give yourself a moment to feel the relief of your larger perspective. Finally, see your problem from God's perspective, unlimited by time, space, or circumstance. Oh, what a difference!!

Remember, God's perspective includes the good that can come from the worst of circumstances. God's perspective includes not only our problem and its solution, but our potential and the potential of those affected by the problem. God sees the fulfillment of his purpose in the matter—a manifestation of God's image within us. What a difference it makes when we look at life and our problems from God's perspective!

Reflection Question:

Think of a problem that you're dealing with right now. What is your perspective? What is God's perspective on the problem? What is God's solution?

_____
_____
_____
_____
_____
_____
_____
_____
_____
_____
_____
_____
_____
_____
_____
_____

_____
_____
_____
_____
_____
_____
_____
_____
_____
_____
_____
_____
_____
_____
_____
_____
_____
_____
_____
_____
_____
_____
_____
_____

Prayer:

Thank you, God. I'm glad that yours is the perspective of the big picture. I get so caught up in the problem that sometimes all I can see is the little picture and its effect on me. I forget that others may be affected too. Help me see the big picture—including not only my needs, but those of others as well. Help me see your answer, not just the problem. Help me see you in the midst of it all.

The Naaman in Me

Rev. Dr. Alfie Wines

Scripture:

Elisha sent a messenger to say to him, "Go, wash yourself seven times in the Jordan, and your flesh will be restored and you will be cleansed." 2 Kings 5:10 NIV

Reflection:

If the truth be told, sometimes, we are our own worst enemy! Naaman, the Syrian commander, was told to wash seven times in the Jordan in order to be healed of leprosy. Naaman wasn't too excited about the idea of washing in the Jordan River. I can imagine that not only was it a blow to his pride, but he felt it would make him look mighty foolish.

Even if Naaman wouldn't listen, someone nearby would. Somebody would listen and convince him to do what the prophet Elisha said to do. To his credit, Naaman listened to the advice of these around him. He washed seven times and was cleansed of his leprosy. What a blessing!

I know there have been times in my life when I have been Naaman. There have been times when I might have missed out on a blessing if someone hadn't convinced me to just try. I remember one time when I couldn't see my way and thought I would skip a semester of seminary—a semester that might have resulted in never completing my degree and never entering ministry. I know that God truly blessed me through the encouraging words Sherry Willis, Dr. Robbie Morgansfield, Dr. Stephen Sprinkle, and Dr. Toni Craven at a time when I really needed encouragement. I am forever grateful.

Reflection Questions:

Have you ever been like Naaman? How did God encourage you? How were you blessed?

_____
_____
_____
_____
_____
_____
_____
_____
_____

Prayer:

Sometimes, Lord, I'm like Naaman, praying for an answer, getting it, and then not liking the answer I received. Lord, help me to be receptive to your answers, even the ones I don't like. When I get answers I don't like, it's because your love is a purifying love, a perfecting love. Even when I get answers I don't like, you are loving me. I don't want to miss out on any of the good things you have for me because I don't like Your instructions or because I don't realize that you've answered my prayer. Help me cooperate with your wisdom and your way. Help me hear and follow through on what you ask of me, even when it feels foolish or I don't like it.

Foolish for God

Rev. Dr. Alfie Wines

Scripture:

Let everything that breathes praise the LORD! Hallelujah!
Psalm 150:6 (God's Word)

Reflection:

I like the story about David dancing his heart out before God and the people of Israel after they finally brought the ark to Jerusalem. Oh, what a wondrous time that must have been! With one failed attempt to bring the ark to Jerusalem behind him, it was a sweet success, a time of unspeakable joy.

Despite his sins, faults, and failures, David was one who truly loved the Lord. His wife, Michal, was really upset with him. She did not understand the extent of his faith in God. Can you imagine the discussion (i.e. argument) that might have ensued regarding his dancing? David made it plain that he was willing to be a fool for God, in spite of her feelings. I imagine he might have tried to help her understand how close he was to God. He might have talked about how he'd grown close to God when he was a mere boy . . .a despised shepherd boy in the days before he was king. Or he might have told her about all of the songs he'd written on his harp in the lonely hours outdoors with the sheep. He might have talked about how much he loved music and the joy of hearing the choir and orchestra he'd organized to praise God lifting their voices in song and instrument as part of the dedication ceremony. Nothing like this had ever happened in Israel before! It was an historic event and David knew, even if Michal didn't, the significance of this occasion.

Perhaps he tried to convince Michal until finally he realized it was useless. Growing up in the palace as the king's daughter, Michal was unable to relate. It created a wound in their relationship that was never healed.

Think about it, here was the king of Israel, dancing totally uninhibited before the entire nation. The entire nation would see him as a real person. No wonder the women sang of him: "Saul has defeated thousands, but David, tens of thousands". Oh, that we too, could learn to be like David--uninhibited, unashamed to express our joy in the Lord.

Reflection Questions:

What feels foolish about your faith in God? Are you willing to trust God anyhow?

_____
_____
_____
_____
_____
_____
_____
_____
_____
_____
_____
_____
_____

_____
_____
_____
_____
_____
_____
_____
_____
_____
_____
_____
_____
_____
_____
_____
_____
_____
_____
_____
_____
_____
_____
_____
_____
_____
_____

Prayer:

Dear God, sometimes believing in and praying to a God I cannot see seems foolish. Yet, my soul cries out for you. Thank you, Lord for making things that appear foolish the wisest things of all! Like David, I foolishly give you all my praise today—today and always!

About the Contributors

Rev. Dr. Georgia Allen is a retired elder in the United Methodist Church. She was the first African American female elder in the Central Texas Conference.

Rev. Denise Bell-Blakely currently serves as Associate Pastor at Meadowbrook United Methodist Church in Fort Worth, Texas. (niecie4him@aol.com)

Rev. Dr. Jacquetta Chambers is an elder who has pastored 5 United Methodist Churches, CEO of Models of Excellence inc, contributor to Women of Color Study Bible, and 2018 Brite Divinity School Distinguished Minister Award, and who presently serves as BCC Senior Chaplain at Texas Health Resources H.E.B.(outclock1@yahoo.com)

April Van Rader served a three-point charge as Senior Pastor of Wesley Chapel, Saints Delight, and New Beginnings in the Waxahachie District. Currently, she is the Senior Pastor of Virtue Ministries International in the Washington D.C. Metro Area. (revapril@gmail.com)

Rev. Alfie Wines, Ph.D. is an elder serving as Senior Pastor of Union Memorial United Methodist Church in the Sandy Community of Coolidge, TX. Dr. Wines writes biblical commentaries, essays, and a guest column (Durable Faith) for the Working Preacher, Craft of Preaching, and Enter the Bible websites sponsored by Luther Seminary. Her online course/book/journal *Take Back Your Life: How to Breakthrough When Life Breaks Your Heart*, and its complementary book, *Seasons: The Stages of Life* will be released in 2018. Her "Bible Study Remix" is on Facebook Live Tuesday evenings 7:00 CST an is available 24/7 after the podcast at: https://www.facebook.com/BibleStudyRemix/. She serves as a Board Member for Equity for Women in the Church and the Alumni Board of Brite Divinity School. She is a member of Daughters of Abraham, a group of Christian,

Jewish, and Muslim women who seek to live and strive for peace. Feel free to reach out:

- Visit my website: dralfiewines.com
- Visit my Facebook (FB) page: https://www.facegook.com/takebackyourlifewithdralfiewines
- Send me an email: dralfie@dralfiewines.com
- Check out my weekly #BibleStudyRemix at https://www.facebook.com/BibleStudyRemix/

If you have been blessed by this book or have questions, we want to hear from you! Feel free to contact us as listed above.

Thank you to the Awesome Team who worked with us on this project:

Andrew Ledell and His Geek Team

DoneForYouTech

http://doneforyoutech.com/

Arian Augustus – Proofreader/Editor

arianaugustus.contently.com

Stephanie Clarke – Editor

smc31810@gmail.com

Denecia Herbert – Publisher

www.shekinahglorypublishing.org

www.ingramcontent.com/pod-product-compliance
Lightning Source LLC
Chambersburg PA
CBHW081331090426
42737CB00017B/3094